John Millington Synge

by DENIS JOHNSTON

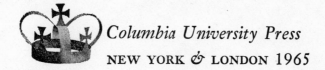

Columbia University Press
NEW YORK & LONDON 1965

COLUMBIA ESSAYS ON MODERN WRITERS is a series of critical studies of English, Continental, and other writers whose works are of contemporary artistic and intellectual significance.

Editor: William York Tindall

Advisory Editors

Jacques Barzun   W.T.H. Jackson   Joseph A. Mazzeo   Justin O'Brien

John Millington Synge is Number 12 of the series.

DENIS JOHNSTON is a Professor at Smith College. He is chairman of the Department of Theatre and Speech.

Copyright © 1965 Columbia University Press
Library of Congress Catalog Card Number: 65–26338
Manufactured in the United States of America

John Millington Synge

John Millington Synge, poet and playwright, the youngest son of a conventional, middle-class Protestant family living in the Dublin suburbs, a rationalist, anticlerical descendant of Anglican bishops, was a writer who gave up Paris for the hills of Wicklow and the bogs of Mayo, preferring the conversation and friendship of tramps and tinkers to the company on the Left Bank.

Although Yeats and Lady Gregory are rightly regarded as the centerpieces of the Irish theatrical renaissance, it was Synge far more than either of these who gave the movement its national quality, and left to the world the type of play that has since become the prototype of Irish folk drama. Yet he managed to get the entire Abbey Theatre Company arrested in Philadelphia, and is still viciously denounced as anti-Irish by most of the grimmer Gaelic enthusiasts.

There are other paradoxical aspects to this strange, sociable hermit—this glum-faced humorist—the associate of a generation of intellectuals, who nevertheless was neither an intellectual nor a nationalist himself. He was a storm-tossed genius, but not a frustrated one. Whether he realized the extent of the international fame that was to be his is something that it is impossible to say: but he certainly gave no signs of caring about it. He was a writer of love passages of enormous lyrical beauty who was never much of a hit with the women he wanted to marry. He was a celebrity about whom the general public, until recently, knew very little . . . thanks to the disapproving attitude of his family toward its principal claim to distinction.

[3]

Apart from scattered references in books on the Abbey Theatre, and the autobiographical essays and correspondence of Yeats, Lady Gregory's diaries, and the mass of undigested misinformation recently deposited in the National Library of Ireland under the name of the *Holloway Papers*, there was comparatively little hard data about John Synge, and practically no objective critical comment on his works during his lifetime, and for a good many years afterwards.

There was a useful but pedestrian work by a Frenchman, Maurice Bourgeois, and there was a volume of letters to his daughter written by one of the author's brothers—Samuel, the missionary—who, one feels, rather reluctantly came to recognize his relative's literary importance about ten years after his death, and who was determined to underline the fact that the youngest Synge had not been an atheist, and did not die of cancer—an affliction that seems to have been regarded in the same spirit of hush-hush as a taste for drink.

Yeats, of course, refers to his protégé in the most appreciative terms, but as none of Yeats's own volumes are indexed, it is not always easy to find the references. Lady Gregory's diaries include sections that deal very fully with Synge, but they have been edited by Lennox Robinson and are not yet before us in anything like their original form. Holloway was inspired with such a personal distaste for everything about Synge and his works that his comments have little factual and no critical value at all. In fact this uncouth, arrogant figure, with the soul of a poet and the instincts of a truant, has been unfortunate in his public image until as recently as 1959.

The published plays were of course widely known, but his innumerable early versions, his manuscripts (when not purchased by Mr. John Quinn of New York), his notebooks, and incoming correspondence were not available for examination until the relations had decided what portions were suitable for release and what were not—which meant, of course, that they were not accessible at all. The family was not only of clerical descent, it was also Anglican and Anglo-Irish, connected professionally with landlords and evictions, and with a profound suspicion of tenants-at-will, of Home Rule, of the theater, and of the robust Catholic girl whom the mottled—if not totally black—sheep of the family had been intending to marry at the untimely moment of his death. One shudders to think what must have happened to the personal papers. Not only have all the incoming love letters from Maire O'Neill vanished, but a number of Synge's own letters to an earlier inamorata, Cherry Matheson, which she was foolish enough to lend to the first of the literary executors, have also dropped into limbo.

The manuscripts, having a salable value, have largely survived, but were it not for Maire O'Neill's prescience in preserving his letters to her, we would know very little about Synge as a person today, apart from what can be deduced from a study of his plays. What we do know from the above is that on the whole he was a poor letter writer, and a technician better suited to the typewriter than to the artifices of courtship.

However, time passes by, and a couple of decades ago the control of Synge's literary estate passed into the hands of his nephew, Edward Stephens, a barrister and a liberal-minded intellectual. Stephens' enthusiasm for his uncle was not only as a writer, but as a member of the family. And who would realize better than a barrister that to state any set of facts adequately it is necessary to begin at the beginning, and to go thoroughly into the background.

The difficulty here is that the Synges are actually a family with a very long record of ecclesiastical service. The family includes several seventeenth-century Anglican bishops, amongst them that peripatetic Bishop of Clonfert, translated to Cloyne, translated to Ferns, translated to Elphin, to whom Swift made one of his most shattering remarks. Swift had invited Edward

[5]

Synge to join him in an attack on the iniquitous Irish government of the day—an activity he could now safely indulge in, having been recently elevated to a diocese. But the Bishop replied that he did not consider the moment opportune. Later maybe, but not now. Not that he did not agree with the Dean of St. Patrick's.

"I understand," said Swift. "Then when your Lordship has got a better bishopric we may expect you to become an honest man." And without waiting for his lordship to recover from this mortal blow, he walked away with the curtain line, "Till then, my Lord, farewell."

As a boy, Stephens had walked the mountains with his Uncle John and enjoyed his table talk. Now he set forth upon a project that soon assumed many of the features of a definitive history of the Synge family, a task in which he persevered until his death in 1955, a date that coincided with a sabbatical from New York University of Professor David Greene. Greene was uninterested in Synges but enormously concerned about Synge, on the basis of which he reached an amicable arrangement with the widow under which he was allowed to do what he liked with the manuscripts provided that Stephens was to be credited as joint author. The result has been the first readable account of Synge's life: *J. M. SYNGE 1871–1909* by Greene and Stephens, to which future inquirers on the subject will be indebted for most of their facts, though not necessarily for their comment on the literary leavings.

"Originality is not enough," writes Synge in one of his notebooks, "unless it has the characteristic of a particular time and locality, and the life that was in it."

This phrase, so useful as the basis of a question in an examination paper, introduces at once the subject of folk material, at a time when to be folksy is widely suspect—and wrongly so. Its acceptance by Synge, when he had already entered upon the life of a *boulevardier* in Paris, saved him from a fate worse than Beckett's. It was Yeats who persuaded him to get out. Yet it is important to remember that there was an essential difference between Yeats's interest in Ireland and Synge's. Ignoring for a moment the political stirrings that had been temporarily aroused in the breast of Yeats by Maud Gonne, the poet's concern about Ireland was literary and mythological. Both Yeats and Synge came from the same sort of Dublin suburban background. Let there be no mistake about that. But to Yeats, Ireland meant two magnificent epic cycles—the Red Branch and the Fenian Sagas, hardly touched by modern hands until the Germans got to work on them during the latter part of the nineteenth century. To Yeats the Irish heritage was Cuchulain, Finn, and Oisin. It was Deirdre and the sons of Usnach. There was nothing folksy about this. It was noble. It was aristocratic. Above all, it was in glorious good taste.

A far cry from this were the peat stacks and half-doors of Aran and Iar Connacht to which Synge directed his footsteps— not with the object of gathering any further information about Queen Maeve and Conchubar, but to get to know a people with a language. This was something better than verse—the language of submerged race speaking in the tongue of their conquerors and infusing it with a music of their own. Synge was never really interested in the political side of the Irish question, and it is the greatest of mistakes to imagine that because he was fascinated by the people of the Fringe he was also concerned about Home Rule. That he was sympathetic toward the aspirations of a community that he liked is understandable, but this does not mean that he considered that they would be any better off under the local gombeen men in Dublin than under the genial supervision of Edward VII. Without any of the sense of patronage that so frequently defeats the gatherer of folklore, Synge loved the spalpeens and tinkers of the glens and the highways, and found them to be good company.

When Yeats came to write a play set in the little white cottages—as he tried on a couple of occasions—it needed Lady Gregory, a landlord, to keep him on the rails. When Synge, on the other hand, starts to write a poetical play on a theme taken from the *Tain Bo Cualgne* he never finishes it at all. As a poet, set against Yeats, he is nowhere. But as an interpreter of the people of Ireland he is in a class by himself. Synge's characters treat both religion and death with an air of brash familiarity that sometimes is mistaken by Protestants for ir-reverence. But it is actually an expression of the fact that the Catholic faith is accepted with the same familiarity as dinner. Describing a tinker at a fair in County Wicklow, which he visited with Jack Yeats, the artist brother of the poet, Synge writes:

Then a woman came up and spoke to the tinker, and they went down the road together into the village. 'That man is a great villain,' said the herd, when he was out of hearing. 'One time he and his woman went up to a priest in the hills and asked him would he wed them for half a sovereign, I think it was. The priest said it was a poor price, but he'd wed them surely if they'd make him a tin can along with it. "I will, faith," said the tinker, "and I'll come back when it's done." They went off then, and in three weeks they came back, and they asked the priest a second time would he wed them. "Have you the tin can?" said the priest. "We have not," said the tinker; "we had it made at the fall of night, but the ass gave it a kick this morning, the way it isn't fit for you at all." "Go on now," said the priest. "It's a pair of rogues and schemers you are, and I won't wed you at all." They went off then, and they were never married to this day.'

This anecdote originally appeared in an article written for the *Manchester Guardian*, which printed it in May, 1907, about six months in advance of the play that Synge built out of it— *The Tinker's Wedding*. It is an example of the factual basis of most of Synge's plots. It gives expression to a down-to-earth mixture of ribaldry, commercialism, and piety that always de-lighted Synge's skeptical heart and required no invention on his part. The tinkers, for all their free-and-easy reputation,

[8]

had a social sense that pointed to marriage as a desirable condition. But only at a price, and in matters of bargaining they were well able to cheat the professional man, who, on his side, was quite prepared to leave them in their condition of mortal sin, if they did not produce enough cash. A smart, practical view of the situation for everybody, and only irreverent or unbelievable in the eyes of those who do not understand them.

Secondly, the passage is interesting as a specimen of the original material out of which Synge created the romanticized dialogue of his plays. The passage itself consists largely of a dialect statement, but it will be noticed that Synge does not attempt to reproduce it phonetically as Shaw loves to do with cockney, and O'Casey half attempts with Dublinese. It no more occurs to Synge to explain its pronunciation to his readers and performers than it would occur to a native Irish speaker to spell Cobh as Cove or Caitlin as Kathleen. Synge was writing for a group of players who knew how to pronounce his words, so he does not bother to substitute apostrophes for terminal g's and d's, or render the names of his characters in a form intelligible to the bourgeoisie, as others have done.

The circumlocution of "It's a pair of rogues and schemers you are" is apparent to all. What is, perhaps, not so apparent is the absence of the plainest of all words, Yes and No.

"Have you the tin can?"

"We have not."

The reason for this is not far to seek. Neither of these two words exists in the Gaelic language. But this fact requires a word of warning. It is a common misconception to suppose that these people are not supposed to be speaking English at all, and that the plays are presenting us with a translation of what they are actually saying. This idea springs from the peculiarities of Synge's dialogue—the flowing participles, the interpolation of words such as "surely" and "himself," the apparent reluctance to give a straight answer to a straight question.

But no question of translation arises. Synge's characters are all speaking the language in which we hear them. At the time at which the plays are supposed to take place, it is doubtful whether many of them knew the Irish language at all. But their parents or grandparents did, and it is from them that these Gaelic grammatical forms have been inherited. "Aye," as a tentative approach to a positive answer, is comparatively easy to find. Not "Yes"—a vulgar Teutonism, but a variant of the more delicate *Oui*. As for "No"—they either say, "I will not," or make use of some Gaelic form that can only be translated in terms such as "It is to be done"—meaning "It has not been done." "Surely" is a direct translation of an expletive or conjunctive form commonly used in the Gaelic. Much the same is true of the expression "Himself" (Ey Fain.)

The danger inherent in the use of this type of speech for theatrical purposes does not appear when Synge employs it, after having distilled it, as it were, from the verbiage of a community in which he was living. It is when it is written in imitation not of the peasantry but of other characters in Irish plays that disaster threatens. Take for example this passage from O'Neill's *Anna Christie*—a so-called Irish part in a very fine American play, where the dialogue of Anna's seaman suitor is not based on observation, but on an acquaintance with the plays of Synge.

"Ah no, it was nothing—aisy for a rale man with guts to him, the like of me. All in the day's work, darlin'. But I won't be denying 'twas a damn narrow squeak. . . . And only for me, I'm telling you, and the great strength and guts is in me, wid be being scoffed by the fishes this minute."

Both as regards structure and vocabulary, the partial use of phonetics, and the intrusion of expressions such as " 'twas a damn narrow squeak," this effort on the part of a major play-

wright to reproduce the language of the country of his fore-
bears, shows the disastrous consequence of attempting to
follow in Synge's footsteps without Synge's ammunition.

"Is that the truth?"
"It is then. For I'm thinking you'll do it surely when himself is
abroad in the dark night after Samhain, stacking turf below in the
bog or drinking poteen with the tinkers of Aghavanagh."

Here is the genuine article. And while it is not essential to
know where Aghavanagh is, it is necessary to know the correct turn of phrase required to answer a question, and what is
actually meant by *Samhain, turf, poteen,* and *tinkers,* in addi-
tion to the proper use of participles. Without wishing to make
any mystery about such matters, let it be said that Aghavanagh
is a mountainy crossroads—the site of a ruined military bar-
racks—in south Wicklow. *Samhain* (pronounced Sòw-en) is
a month of the year commencing in the late fall. *Turf* is the
Irish word for peat. *Poteen* (pronounced Pòt-yeen) is illegal
whisky—moonshine. A tinker is not a gypsy, although like the
gypsy he is an itinerant, a breeder of large families, a pest
wherever he camps—with his donkeys, his colored carts, and
his wild-looking girls and fortunetelling crones. Unlike the
gypsy he is indigenous to the country, and is dignified by having an ostensible trade—the making and mending of pots and
pans. Hence the word, tin-ker, and his excuse for entering
people's yards, outhouses, and private driveways under a legitimate cloak of inquiring after broken kitchenware.

When we turn to the plays, to study Synge's use of passages
of dialect of the kind quoted above, we may notice that there
is a development in his technique over the years during which
he was working. The type of dialogue now familiar as Synge's
did not spring into existence fully equipped from the first
moment of its appearance, but is something that the dramatist
experimented with from play to play, until it reached its final

[11]

flowering in *The Playboy*. Indeed, the earliest form in which we find it is perilously like some of the parodies of "the Abbey play" that have appeared in skits from time to time. That it is susceptible to parody is not necessarily to its discredit, but there is little doubt that as a type of writing it had a style that could be carried too far.

The mists rolling down the bog, and the mists again and they rolling up the bog, and hearing nothing but the wind crying out in the bits of broken trees were left from the great storm, and the streams roaring with the rain.

This depressing weather report is of the type that laughingly came to be known as "The mist that does be on the bog." It comes from Synge's first play, *In the Shadow of the Glen*, where the response appearing in the text:

I've heard tell it's the like of that talk you do hear from men, and they after being a great while on the back hills

had only to be altered very slightly ("on the back hills" to "in the back stalls") to constitute a deadly comment on the overuse of the style.

The glen in question is usually recognized as Glenmalure—a long, picturesque cleft in the Wicklow mountains running from near Rathdrum to the watershed, across which one can travel on foot down the reverse slope into south Kildare and the plains of Carlow. At Drumgoff Bridge an old military road descends into this valley from the direction of Laragh and the Seven Churches of Glendalough, and winds off over the opposite slope to Aghavanagh, already referred to. Near this bridge, energetic young hikers break away nowadays from the metaled road, and begin the ascent of Lugnaquilla, the highest mountain in Leinster. But Synge's characters are not hikers nor climbers—nor is it likely that they greatly appreciate the scenery.

There is a widespread notion that most of Synge's plays are

set in the Aran Islands. Actually *Riders to the Sea* is the only island play, while *The Playboy* is the only other work that is set in Connaught. Synge places more of his plays in County Wicklow than anywhere else, and what he has to say about the Leinster vagrants is, on the whole, more fully observed and familiarly expressed than are his comments on the western people.

In the Shadow of the Glen is not only noted for the wealth of meteorological lore embodied in its lines:

It's a wild night, lady of the house to be out tramping the roads and the rain falling.

It is also remembered for the hysterical attacks that were made on it, when it was first produced, by a number of prominent separatists in the National movement—notably Arthur Griffith. The arguments advanced against the play were sufficiently farfetched to confirm the suspicion that the real objections lay deeper in the psychology of the play's opponents. The play was denounced as being pagan—the offspring of the tale of the Widow of Ephesus, related by Petronius. This brilliant, but ghoulish little story is one that has been retold in recent years by Christopher Fry under the title *A Phoenix Too Frequent*. It concerns a supposedly model relict who gives away the body of her husband to be hung on a gibbet in order to save the life of her next lover, a young Roman soldier who had been spending the evening with her when he should have been guarding the gibbet. There is another, much simpler variant of the story that concerns a widow who sits in a churchyard fanning her deceased husband's grave, because, it transpires, she has made a promise not to remarry until the earth is dry over his bones. This has been made use of by Donagh MacDonagh in *Happy As Larry*. Neither of these other plays has been assailed on anti-Christian grounds—although it has been suggested more than once that the Fry play presents the

[13]

impossible combination of light comedy dialogue followed by a Charles Addams denouement.

The odd thing about the objection to Synge's play is that it actually bears no resemblance to Petronius's story at all, apart from the fact that it opens with a widow waking her husband. The play in its substance has much more in common with Yeats's *The Land of Heart's Desire*—a blameless play in Irish eyes. Indeed, if any comparisons are to be made on the basis of plot, it would be much more to the point to look on Synge's play as *The Land of Heart's Desire* in the Bartokean Minor, with the tramp taking the place of the fairy child, and the family sitting down around the fire afterwards, delighted with the fact that they have seen the last of that Bride.

This analogy is not offered in jest. Although no suggestion is made that Synge had Yeats's play in mind, the sentiments are very much the same, although one dramatist was concerned at the time with fairies, while the other preferred tramps and tinkers.

In both plays we find the theme of escape—escape from the fear of growing old. The Land of Faery is a place

> Where nobody gets old and godly and grave,
> Where nobody gets old and crafty and wise,
> Where nobody gets old and bitter of tongue.

What Synge's tramp promises to the woman is as follows:

. . . it's not from the like of them you'll be hearing a tale of getting old like Peggy Cavanagh, and losing the hair off you, and the light of your eyes, but its fine songs you'll be hearing when the sun goes up, and there'll be no old fellow wheezing, the like of a sick sheep, close to your ear.

And so they go off together, not necessarily to a life of sin but to one of liberty. And the old man—who, after all, cannot help being old—settles down with a bottle by the fire, and with a sense of peace that suggests that he may be well able to look after himself in spite of his wife's prophecies to the con-

trary. In the same spirit of relaxation he invites his rustic rival
to join him.

I was thinking to strike you, Michael Dara; but you're a quiet man,
God help you, and I dont mind you at all. Your good health,
Michael Dara.

Such a situation as the final curtain for a play ostensibly
about the noble peasant arouses a set of confused values that
is not unheard of in the theater of today, but was before its
time in 1903. Here we have a play about marriage and temptation, about an old man and a younger rival, with a taste of
Deirdre about it—another aspect of a well-loved theme that
is as Irish as the shamrock and not Greek at all. But where are
the moral values? We know where we are with Tristram and
with Naisi. They sin and they suffer for it, and that's all right
so long as it is clear to everyone that they do sin. This is what
tragedy consists of—sufferings for misbehavior, or because of
some fatal flaw. We know what side we are on and who the
author intends us to root for. But who can say, after seeing
this work of Synge's, how the moral chips are supposed to
fall—if indeed, they fall anywhere at all? She escapes, yet she
resents being turned out. The old man ought to hit the lover
and should find trouble in getting on without his helpmeet.
But he anticipates no difficulties whatever on the latter score,
and settles down to a drink with his rival, because—if you
please—he likes him.

Such a play offends against all the canons of good melodrama, while looking like a melodrama. Worse than this, it
seems to come up with the antisocial suggestion that, while
women are entitled to be as free as the air, as from the date
of their Ibsenite liberation—and indeed should be encouraged
in this direction—men can probably get on without them. This
is not a Greek idea. It is much more like Deirdre with a Shavian twist. As for this Barriesque aversion to growing old, it
was to be an experience that Synge was never to have but

that Yeats was to carry with added distinction. Without old age, what would Yeats have been? A beekeeper on Innisfree. With it, Synge would probably have had a tempestuous marriage that might or might not have contributed to the quality of his plays. But such speculation is unprofitable. All that can be said is that the play offers no justification for any fear of old age.

In expressing our pleasure in this strange little play we need not be taken as subscribing to any such sentiments. The point is that audiences that are invited to form their own judgments are usually irritated audiences, and tend to abuse the author. This is particularly so in the case of critics like Arthur Griffith—a man who was very far from being a fool, but whose firm dedication to the idea of a new conception of Ireland had made him sensitive about any portrayal of the peasant that might turn out to be an ascendancy sneer. Exactly the same reaction might be expected in this country today amongst Civil Righters toward any white man's play that appeared to make fun of the colored races, whether or not it was so intended.

And here is the point with regard to Synge. Had he been interested in the people in a tourist's manner, he would doubtless have written some appreciative rubbish about them along the lines of *Man of Aran* that would have raised no protests at all from the Nationalists, but a general feeling of contempt amongst the islanders. As it was, Synge did not feel himself to be in any way apart from the tinkers and the tramps of Ireland, and would no more fear to write about their faults and their rascalities than he would hesitate to describe those of Crosthwaite Park, Dun Laoghaire. The only pity is that he allowed himself to be taken aback by some of the nonsensical criticism of his earlier work, and that he censored himself in consequence, or worse still, wrote some disastrous program notes, which are always a mistake—especially when one is not at all clear what the trouble is about.

One of the most curious pieces of censorship is to be found

in his essay "The People of the Glens," which first appeared in the magazine *The Shanachie* in 1907, and has a significant final paragraph, which was deleted when the essay was reprinted in the *Collected Works*—the *Playboy* row being, no doubt, the reason. This is what he says—and as an expression of realistic appreciation in an entirely unpatronizing vein, it strikes the ear today as being far ahead of its time.

The younger people of these glens are not so interesting as the old men and women; and though there are still many fine young men to be met with among them who are extraordinarily gifted and agile, it too often happens, especially in the more lonely places, that the men under thirty are badly built, shy, and despondent. Even among the older people, whose singular charm I have tried to interpret, it should perhaps be added that it is possible to find many individuals who are far from admirable in temper or in morals. One would hardly stop to assert a fact so obvious if it had not become the fashion in Dublin, quite recently, to reject a fundamental doctrine of theology, and to exalt the Irish peasant into a type of absolute virtue, frugal, self-sacrificing, valiant, and I know not what. There is some truth in this estimate, yet it is safer to hold with the theologians that, even west of the Shannon, the heart of man is not spotless, for though the Irish peasant has many beautiful virtues, it is idle to assert that he is totally unacquainted with the deadly sins, or with any minor rogueries. He has, however, it should never be forgotten, a fine sense of humour and the greatest courtesy. When a benevolent visitor comes to his cottage, seeking a sort of holy family, the man of the house, his wife, and all their infants, too courteous to disappoint him, play their parts with delight. When the amiable visitor, however, is once more in the boreen, a storm of good-tempered irony breaks out behind him that would surprise him could he hear it. This irony I have heard many times in places where I have been intimate with the people, and I have always been overjoyed to hear it. It shows that, in spite of relief-works, commissions, and patronising philanthropy—that sickly thing—the Irish peasant, in his own mind, is neither abject nor servile.

This is an estimate that is even truer today, and might profitably be included in some of the contemporary guide books. All that one need take exception to is the fact that in 1910— after Synge's death—it was thought politic to leave the passage out.

[17]

There are still a few old people on the Aran Islands who remember Synge, and many more who are prepared to repeat what they heard about him from their elders. Probably the most significant tribute that can be paid to his memory is the fact that on the whole they speak well of him—which is more than can be said for another visitor, Robert Flaherty, the film director, whose sentimental enthusiasms for everything about the islanders would appear at first blush to be more flattering to the ego than Synge's sardonic understanding. But however flattering it may seem, no community enjoys being pressed to assume the clothes and practices of fifty years ago for the purpose of making it seem more picturesque than it is today. Aran men do not wear funny tam-o-shanters, nor attempt to harpoon sunfish, nor fish off the top of the cliffs of Dun Aengus, and they see no point—apart from a financial one—in pretending that they do. On the other hand, *Riders to the Sea* may not be quite the sort of play that a man from Kilmurvy would write about his family, but there are many things in it that he understands. Above all, he appreciates the fact that it does not insist that he is picturesque.

The Greek analogy is legitimate here. *Riders to the Sea* has a classical unity and a completeness that makes one aware of the fact that in a sense it has ended before it begins. What happens is inevitable, and in this fact resides the real nub of its tragedy. There is no need for us to make up our minds whether or not we like the doomed Bartley, or even whether we are at all sorry for his predecessor, Michael, whose clothes are laid out on the table. It is not Bartley's death over which we grieve, nor even the death of Man. Everybody must die sooner or later—a fact which, as a rule, is a matter for congratulation rather than the reverse. "Sooner or later" is the operative part of the statement here, and the pity of the play is that in this community the young tend to go before the old.

In the big world, says Maurya, the old people do be leaving things after them for their sons and children, but in this place it is the young men do be leaving things behind for them that do be old.

Riders is probably the most frequently performed of all Synge's plays—principally by amateurs, and most frequently of all in schools and colleges. It appears to present no difficulties in casting, and the sentiments to which it gives voice do not seem to offer any obvious problems either in interpretation or direction. That it does not usually manage to convey the required sensation of catharsis but merely one of depression is probably owing to the fact that both these impressions are wrong—usually as wrong as the costuming.

Riders to the Sea is not a play about a tiresome community that insists on going on with its fishing in spite of inadequate equipment and a continuing disregard for the weather reports. It is true that one son after another gets drowned, and it is not difficult to experience a certain mild irritation with Bartley—the baby of the family—who continues to wave aside all warnings, until he finishes up precisely where one would expect to find him—laid out on the table. And then one has to put up with an outburst of passionate mourning with which the performance usually ends. Without a suggestion of suspense, or some illumination of character or motivation, it is usually a pleasure when it is over. And one asks oneself how can such an expression of the obvious be put in the category of the great—except as some formal gesture of respect for peasants, for Ireland, and for Synge?

The point is, of course, that *Riders to the Sea* is a much better play than this kind of treatment suggests, and is far from easy either to cast or to perform. A superficial production of the type that has been mentioned has nothing to do with the classical form, but makes it instead into an inadequate Faust story, in which the victim goes to his predicted fate without ever having had an evening of love in return for his pains. On this basis, it would be a very much better play if Bartley were not going to the mainland to sell horses but to savor the stews of that sophisticated Babylon, the city of Galway. This would certainly give it something of the pious Christian touch that, prior to Goethe, was a necessity to any Faust story. If the production suggests that a matter of free choice is involved, and that Bartley goes on in spite of the warnings that a more sensible son would observe, it can be nothing but a Faust story. Yet whoever heard of a Faust who barters his future to attend a horse fair?

But *Riders to the Sea* is neither pious nor basically Christian. It is Orestean, and in the true Greek tradition, where no moral choice at all is offered to the characters. The sea—not the Gods—is the source of the law in this play, and there is no escape from it. The play is not trying to tell us how sad it is to have a son drowned—especially if he happens to be the last. We might be expected to know this already, and no play, classical or otherwise, can be great if it merely tells us something that we have expected from the start, without even an element of surprise in the telling.

What the play does tell us is the effect of the inevitable on these people, and what, if anything, man's answer to the Gods should be. In order to appreciate the point of the last two pages it is necessary to understand two or three unmelodramatic and very Synge-like assumptions: first, that there is no moral element whatever involved in these people pursuing the life that is theirs, whether or not it must end in death. All life ends in death, and one does not say to a dying man, "There you are, now. This is what you get for having been born. I told you so, but you wouldn't listen." This is a correct Faust conclusion—and it is a fatuous one without an afterlife in either heaven or hell. But nobody has any data on Bartley's final destination. The play is about him being drowned—not about his character. So it is clearly the gods whom we are up against—not a moral judgment.

The dilemma is that of Orestes, who by the law of life is

bound to avenge his father. But by the law of life he must not kill his mother. What is he to do, except protest against the law of life?

So, also, Bartley must go down to the sea, and if in doing so he meets his end, there is no element of "I told you so" about it. His mother must accept the situation. But there is an answer that she may give, an answer that is the point of the play.

They're all gone now [she says], and there isn't anything more that the sea can do to me . . . I'll have no call now to be crying and praying when the wind breaks from the south, and you can hear the surf is in the east, and the surf is in the west, making a great stir with the two noises, and they hitting one on the other. I'll have no call now to be going down and getting Holy Water in the dark nights after Samhain, and I wont care what way the sea is when the other women will be keening . . . it's a great rest I'll have now, and it's time, surely. It's a great rest I'll have now, and great sleeping in the long nights after Samhain, if it's only a bit of wet flour we do have to eat, and maybe a fish that would be stinking.

These expressions of human dignity under the buffetings of life are not wails of anguish, nor are they even projections of the stoicism of Job. They are man's answer to Heaven, and should be played as such. They give tongue to much the same idea that is to be found in a minor key in *Waiting for Godot*, where Vladimir protests

. . . we are blessed in this, that we happen to know the answer. Yes, in this immense confusion one thing alone is clear. We are waiting for Godot to come—or for night to fall. We have kept our appointment and that's an end to that. We are not saints, but we have kept our appointment. How many people can boast as much?

This is a universal answer, the significance of which we are finding extremely pertinent since the coming of the Atomic Age. Yet here it is expressed in 1903. But there is also a more special element that Synge dramatizes in the course of the play which also contains great theatrical possibilities. Bartley is drowned, but this is not by chance. He does not fall casually into the water, nor does he go down with some ship. It is the rearing of the horse behind that knocks him off the cliff. And who is riding on the rearmost horse? The ghost of his brother Michael.

Here we notice another important element of the folk attitude toward the dead themselves. In some ways it resembles the popular attitude toward the fairies that is so vividly underlined in *Heart's Desire*. In Irish eyes the fairies are not Shakespearean or Gilbertean creatures,

> Tripping hither, tripping thither,
> Nobody knows why or whither.

They are malevolent beings who steal children away with specious promises of better times. So, too, the dead want company. It is the ghostly Michael who is the killer of his younger brother—for reasons that lie deep in the Irish psychology, and are the basis of a universal fear of the dead. Count Dracula presents us with a vulgarized version of the same idea; but debased or not, the story is the same: in the half-world of the grave, there is a host of conjured spirits who would, if they could, make us like themselves.

That the dead are not to be trusted is an idea to be found even in that most sinister of spiritualistic farces—*Blithe Spirit* by Noel Coward. In Synge's play the sea is the executioner, but the horses make the occasion—the horses that must be sold at the fair but that carry the dead no less than the living. Herein we find that union of causation and denouement that is the sure sign of a well-constructed play. There is no escape, owing to the fact that the Urge is its own Consequence.

The play is misinterpreted if it ends in a screaming match of competitive grief—or indeed in a performance that suggests stoic indifference.

Bartley will have a fine coffin out of the white boards, and a deep grave surely. What more can we want than that? No man at all can be living for ever, and we must be satisfied.

The priest is not right when he says

> . . . she'll be getting her death with crying and lamenting . . . Herself does be saying prayers half through the night, and the Almighty God won't leave her destitute.

God does leave her destitute. And it is her own dead who bring it about—a double blow to which she gives the only answer, even though nobody listens.

> It's life of a young man to be going on the sea, and who would listen to an old woman with one thing, and she saying it over?

Riders to the Sea is hard to cast, and needs to be very subtly interpreted; otherwise it is liable to appear as a dreary little suspense story without any suspense.

The Well of the Saints and *The Tinker's Wedding* are plays that are not very well known on the stage. This neglect requires some explanation, since both of them are on themes of greater interest—one would imagine—than the arguable subject matter of *The Playboy*, which comedy, for all its stormy history, has turned out to be a very popular item.

Both plays may be taken as examples of the fact that few Irish dramatists are really good craftsmen, and that they usually win their laurels by accident and by dialogue rather than by any technical artfulness in their design. This is not necessarily to their discredit, and it is as plainly seen in the case of Sean O'Casey and Behan as it ever was with Synge. Yeats himself has left us two versions of his play *The Shadowy Waters*, in neither of which can much sense be made of his stage directions, for all the magnificence of the language. (Take for example the final moment when the hero is expected to wrap the heroine's hair about him, as a harp "begins to burn as with fire.") The consistently good technicians of the Abbey Theatre were Lennox Robinson and George Shiels, and who hears much of the plays of either of these writers now?

[23]

The Well of the Saints is concerned with an idea that has also been touched on by Ibsen, O'Neill, and H. G. Wells—that it is probably better not to have one's eyes opened. There are all the elements of a good satirical farce in this paradox, and Synge makes the most of some of them in the early stages of his play. It is easy to smile at the obvious conflict between the pictures the blind beggars have of each other and the reality that we—the knowing ones—can see before us on the stage. At the same time not everybody in the play is hideous, and some of the other characters do match up well enough with the imaginary picture that each tramp has of the other. The point of the satire is not, therefore, as Beckett would probably have it, that an opening of the eyes discloses a world that is universally loathsome, but merely that Martin and Mary Doul are each unfortunate in a particular spouse. This gives the satire a limited application. At the same time, the author attempts to inflate what is clearly the material for a good one-act play into the three-act form, with the result that a promising short play becomes a tenuous long one, and in the course of which one good point, acceptable at 9 P.M., has more than exhausted itself before ten.

According to Mr. Holloway, the general feeling in the company about *The Well of the Saints* was that it made them sick. Holloway, as an authority upon any subject, with the possible exception of acting, is not only tasteless but is factually unreliable. But Willie Fay, the Abbey's first director, was a sound man of the theater with a lot of good comment about most of the early plays, and he made the point that any play in which all the characters, without exception, express themselves in a vein of unrelieved bad temper tends to make an audience feel the same way about the play. Although this comment on the dialogue of *The Well* is exaggerated, there is something in what Fay says about the absence of Synge's customary good humor from this work, and this lack may be one of the principle elements that has stood in the way of its popularity. It has two superb beggars of the type that only Synge could create, a foolish fellow who is a prototype for Pegeen's Sean Keogh, a priggish saint, and a likely young woman called Molly Byrne—not to be confused with Mary Byrne in *The Tinker*. (Wicklow is full of Byrnes.) But all the other characters are as superfluous as the two spare acts.

The other play—*The Tinker's Wedding*—is based on the story, already quoted, about the vagrants' thirst for respectability, and in its picture of the conflict between lay and clerical rapacity it should ring a very loud bell, not only in Irish hearts but in many another too. One wonders, therefore, why this is the only play of Synge that has never been performed by the Abbey Theatre. It would certainly have caused a riot if presented in Dublin, but this fact would not have been regarded as sufficient reason for suppressing it in the healthy heyday of the Irish dramatic movement. What, then, is there about it that made it different from *The Playboy*, which was at once recognized as a work of art over which it would be worthwhile to have a row? Yeats and Lady Gregory were good generals in their ability to pick battlefields where they had a chance of victory, and in declining combat on ground where they would be at a disadvantage.

While *The Well of the Saints* is predated for some reason "one or more centuries ago," *The Tinker's Wedding* is dateless, and is also undefined so far as geography is concerned, although it is clear from the text that it must also be a Wicklow play. The printed version is introduced by one of Synge's rare prefaces, from which one gathers that he is anxious to reassure his coming audiences that nothing serious is intended and that they may lean back and be prepared to laugh.

Of the things which nourish the imagination humour is one of the most needful, and it is dangerous to limit or destroy it. . . . I do not think that these country people, who have so much humour

[25]

themselves, will mind being laughed at without malice, as the people in every country have been laughed at in their own comedies.

Such a preface is of course a fair indication that the author is expecting trouble, and hopes to forestall it. This was not on account of the play's noisy anticlericalism, but because it calls, quite unnecessarily, for violent hands to be laid on one of the clergy. This is going too far. However much the public might enjoy the character of the priest that the play depicts, he must not be gagged and tied up in a sack—a fact that Yeats knew but Synge apparently did not regard as fatal. Apart from the uncalled for complication, the play is basically an expression of the mother-in-law joke—an old favorite in the music halls, though here reduced, in the best tradition of Swift's Lilliput, to the language and level of the tinkers—if, indeed, this can be regarded as a reduction.

For all the carefree and supposedly untrammeled life of the tinkers, we here discover that they too have social levels and their own variety of snobbery.

. . . I do be thinking I'd have a right to be going off to the rich tinkers do be travelling from Tibradden to the Tara Hill . . .

There is also a very professional view of the economic sanctions of matrimony:

If I didn't marry her, she'd be off walking to Jaunting Jim maybe at the fall of night; and it's well yourself knows there isn't the like of her for getting money and selling songs to the men.

But marriage is also something of a status symbol:

I've as good a right to a decent marriage as any speckled female does be sleeping in the black hovels above, would choke a mule.

In all these respects *The Tinker* is not a wild Romany romp, but is a parody of a very middle-class play, with the thirst for respectability as the dominating motive. It anticipates in an amusing way many of the features of Joyce's marriage in the Caxton Hall in 1932, after some years of irregularity, and

[26]

several children, although in Joyce's case the outside element that sparked it off was not the arrival of a mother-in-law, but of a rich American daughter-in-law.

The play also depicts, not unsympathetically, the rapacity and practicality of the clergy, who are not so unworldly as to be unaware of the presence of the opposite sex:

a piece of glass to shield your windows when you do be looking out and blinking at the girls

but also are quite prepared to allow their parishioners to re- main living in mortal sin indefinitely if they fail to produce the necessary cash to pay for a sacrament. None of this would probably evoke any public dissent in the city of Dublin, were it not for the further incident demanded by the script—that violent hands are laid on the *Soggarth Aroon*.

The Irish are fully aware of certain *lacunae* in the social setup, and are not so unsophisticated as to be shocked at a quantitative view of some of the comforts of the Church.

To think you'd be putting deceit on me, and telling lies to me, and I going to marry you for a little sum wouldn't marry a child.

Indeed, it was President de Valera—a very perceptive and reasonable man in many ways—who is alleged to have pointed out that in England you may say what you like so long as you do the right thing, but in Ireland you may do what you like so long as you say the right thing. To lay violent hands on the clergy, however, takes the matter a step further, and amounts both to doing and saying the wrong thing at the same time.

Although it might be bearable to have it reported in the course of a play that a priest had been assaulted in an un- dignified manner, there is, in the words of Pegeen Mike, "a great gap between a gallous story and a dirty deed." No burn- ings of the published play took place, but Synge calls for its actual performance on the stage. This incident is something that might be cut or ignored were it not for the further fact that the scene is only one aspect of an ineffective denouement in which one feels that the author's bad temper on the subject of holy men has once more got the better of him, and hurried him into an ending that is not up to the level of the theme of the play.

What Mary Casey would probably have done in the absence of the necessary twenty shillings is something that occasionally happens where education is involved and the necessary funds are short. She would probably have slyly hinted at a visit to the Protestant parson as an alternative. We hear quite a lot about this rival cleric and his family in the course of the play:

. . . I'll sell the can to the parson's daughter below, a harmless poor creature would fill your hand with shillings for a brace of lies.

It is probable that all questions of economics would have vanished miraculously had there been any possibility of a Dutch auction between the faiths for the privilege of performing the desired ceremony—a real tinker's solution. But here it is legitimate to suspect that there was a limit to Synge's anti-clericalism where the persuasion of his own family was concerned. He was probably more afraid of his mother than of Michael Byrne's, and so this amusing and quite logical conclusion was dodged. In the absence of a better ending, it was not a play that was worth a riot, and Yeats and Lady Gregory were probably right in biding their time for a more worthy occasion—which they got.

It is interesting, however, to note the development of Synge's dialogue from the foggy dew of the earlier plays.

. . . . if it's flighty you are itself, you're a grand, handsome woman, the glory of tinkers, the pride of Wicklow, the Beauty of Ballinacree. I wouldn't have you lying down and you lonesome to sleep this night in a dark ditch when the spring is coming in the trees; so let you sit down there by the big bough, and I'll be telling you the finest story you'd hear any place from Dundalk to Ballinacree, with great queens in it, making themselves matches from the start to the end, and they with shiny silks on them the length of the day, and white shifts for the night.

Here is a preliminary appearance of a word—shift—that was to be the occasion for the shrillest part of the outburst over *The Playboy*. It was insisted by a section of the rioters that no such unseductive undergarment was fit to be mentioned in public on a decent Irish stage. This, however, is just another example of the way in which the mob usually spoils its own case by picking the wrong reason. There is another passage in *The Playboy*—also a development of an earlier excursion into mild indecency in *The Tinker's Wedding*—that might have served as a better occasion for a screaming match.

In *The Tinker's Wedding*, the passage runs as follows:

If I go, I'll be telling old and young you're a weathered heathen savage, Sarah Casey, the one did put down the head of the parson's cabbage to boil in the pot with your clothes, and quenched the flaming candles on the throne of God the time your shadow fell within the pillars of the chapel door.

Nothing much here, except abuse. But see what Pegeen's abuse of the Widow Quin can become in the next play:

Doesn't the world know you reared a black ram at your own breast, so that the Lord Bishop of Connaught felt the elements of a Christian, and he eating it after in a kidney stew.

It was in London after the playwright's death, at a two-thirty matinee performance in November, 1909, that *The Tinker's Wedding* first appeared on the stage. In the United States there was a New York production by the Washington Square Players in 1919, from which event no disturbances are reported, save the sputtering of carbon arcs.

In *The Playboy of the Western World*, which first appeared in the Abbey Theatre in January, 1907, we find the final application of the various experiments with dialogue and construction that have gone before. It is also of some significance that this is the first of Synge's plays in which a major role is written for a mettlesome young actress. Irish drama to this day is surprisingly short in good leading roles for young women. Character women there are in abundance, and character juveniles too. But precious little for the like of Miss Siobhan McKenna—apart from Pegeen Mike. This new aspect of Synge's work coincides with his courtship of a member of the company—Miss Maire O'Neill—or to give her real name, Molly Allgood. An elder sister, Sara Allgood (or Algood, as she is misspelled in the Theatre's earliest programs) had been appearing in the productions of the National Theatre Society since it had opened in the Abbey. Sara had been a protégé of William Fay, and at an early age had acquired an international reputation as a member of the company, and a pre-emptive right to most of the female dramatic leads. Actually, in retrospect she was not as great an actress as she has been painted, being inclined to sing her lines, thanks to the temptation of a melodious voice, and although she was full of temperament, she was not overendowed with intelligence. However, on the stage, playing with a repertory company, she was as firm as a rock, and a thoroughly reliable performer. Offstage she was generally regarded as rather tiresome.

Her young sister, Molly, who began her adult life as a shopgirl in Grafton Street, was exactly the opposite. A charmer in private life—humorous, intelligent, and generous to a fault—she could be an absolute devil on the stage, if the spirit moved her. Like most of the Irish players she worked best on her nerves. A long run would bore her. Before many weeks had passed she would be amusing herself by playing the fool, and then anything might happen.

One of the most characteristic incidents concerning Molly O'Neill occurred toward the end of her career, when she was taking the part—of all things—of one of the neighbors in a film version of *Riders to the Sea*. It was a Friday, late in the afternoon, and a week's shooting had almost concluded. For a time it had seemed as if, thanks to various delays, the work would go over into another week, but great efforts were being made by the director to speed up the final shots—much to the disgust of the little group of Irish players, who, like Molly, had been employed by the week and were now soon to be out of work.

As the final take ground under way, and the clock approached the deadline, Molly was standing in the forefront of the neighbors, keening away over the body of Bartley, when slowly, with an air of finality, her heavy red Aran skirt descended to the floor, leaving Keening-Woman-One in mid shot, clad in a shawl and a pair of unbecoming bloomers.

"Cut," screamed the assistant director.

"Retake," shouted the cameraman.

The director was speechless, and Molly was most apologetic. But by the time safety pins had been sent for and inserted at appropriate places, it was too late for a retake, and everybody was called again for Monday.

She was, of course, a Catholic—a matter of no surprise to Synge's mother and brothers, who had anticipated just such an outcome of his association with those play actors of the National Theatre. Greene and Stephens describe how, shortly after the new theater was opened, Synge left his mother's house in Kingstown and went to live in the suburb of Rathmines in part to be nearer to his love. He took her for walks from Bray, and out of the welter of his first successful love encounter, his work-in-progress took on a new rhapsodic note that had been absent from his earlier dialogue.

Let you wait, to hear me talking, till we're astray in Erris, when Good Friday's by, drinking a sup from a well, and making mighty kisses with our wetted mouths, or gaming in a gap of sunshine, with yourself stretched back unto your necklace, in the flowers of the earth.

Yet it was an undemonstrative and discreet courtship, as those of the company who remember it have been heard to say. Synge would be found sitting silently in a corner of the

Green Room staring into the fire as some play was concluding on the stage. Presently Molly would sweep in, dressed in her street clothes, and without as much as a glance in his direction, she would exchange a boisterous word or two with those present, and then leave—ostensibly for home. Presently Synge would rise, pick up his heavy stick, and bid them all a terse goodnight. Everybody knew that he would catch up with her on O'Connell Bridge, yet the absurd convention remained that nobody was supposed to know—an affectation of his to which the girl good-humoredly subscribed. The fact that they never married may, perhaps, be regarded as fortunate so far as their romance was concerned. They had not the makings of a well-matched couple.

As already mentioned, Synge wrote one of his few prefaces as an introduction to the printed text of *The Tinker's Wedding*, in which he not only urged his audiences to relax and to laugh, but also provided us with some indication of his views on what the proper function of the theater ought to be.

We should not go to the Theatre as we go to a drug store or a Bar, but as we would to a good dinner. . . . The drama, like the symphony, does not teach or prove anything.

If we try to make them perform any such function, as Ibsen does, Synge insists that the plays as works of art are dated as soon as they are written.

. . . . the whole people—he goes on to say—from the tinkers to the clergy, have still a life, and view of life, that are rich and genial and humorous.

While it is understandable that he should hope to forestall any more manifestations of what he calls the "morbid" reactions aroused by *In the Shadow of the Glen*, it is not easy to subscribe wholeheartedly to the last part of this statement. The objections to *The Shadow* may have been misdirected but they were hardly morbid. Nor could the view of life of the tinkers or the clergy be reasonably regarded as either rich or genial.

Another of these prefaces is attached to the first edition of *The Playboy*, and was evidently inspired by suggestions from the same hostile quarters that no peasant from any part of Ireland—east or west—ever spoke as Synge's characters spoke. On the contrary, he says, he has never used more than one or two words that he has not heard amongst the country people of Ireland, or spoken in his nursery before he could read the newspapers.

It is probably true that he had heard all the words he uses, though probably not in the same order. Synge undoubtedly glorifies the language.

In a good play every speech should be as fully flavored as a nut or an apple. . . . Those of us who wish to write, start (in Ireland) with a chance that is not given to writers in places where the spring time of local life has been forgotten, and the harvest is a memory only, and the straw has been turned into bricks.

The setting of *The Playboy* is described as a country public house, or "shebeen." It can hardly be both, in the sense of being a speak-easy, since a pub is a legal place for drinking while a shebeen is not. Its illegality probably consists in functioning at forbidden hours—restrictions which in turn are rendered pointless, since every customer, were he to come by road, would have come from a distance of over three miles, thereby constituting himself a "bona fide traveler" entitled to a drink at any time.

The lady of the house bears an honorable surname for the west of Ireland, Flaherty, but is known as Pegeen Mike to indicate that as amongst the many Flaherties, she is Michael's daughter. It does not appear why she needs a dispensation in order to marry Sean Keogh, but presumably it is on the grounds of some relationship. Were he her first cousin, for instance, a dispensation would be necessary.

The story line, Synge tells us, is taken from a newspaper story of the time, and it is pure nonsense to write about the theme as if it were a satire on peasant duplicity and love of crime. Christy Mahon—a name pronounced as if almost of one syllable, Maan—is not at all anxious to describe his act of violence to begin with. Nor has he any idea that it might evoke any expressions of admiration. Indeed, it is only dragged out of him by a burst of temper and the fear that he is going to get hit over the head by Pegeen's broom.

He sees himself as a respectable, God-fearing lad, unaddicted to the use of weapons, and believing his own story about the row with his Da—the lamentable result of unendurable provocation. There is nothing peculiarly Irish or even rustic in an interest in a good tale of violence, particularly if committed at a distance. The presents from the local girls with which the second act begins, may perhaps be a little premature, but there is nothing odd in the fact that Christy is not handed over to the police. This would have been a matter of social tradition, and there are plenty of precedents—headed by the celebrated case of Lynchehaun referred to by Joyce. So far as crimes of violence were concerned, an elaborate game was played with the police, based upon a long tradition of political agitation, and the date of the play is clearly fixed by Philly's question

Were you off east, young fellow, fighting bloody wars for Kruger and the freedom of the Boers?

Where the play usually goes off the rails in production is in the sudden change of heart in the last act, where Pegeen turns upon him in the presence of the crowd and orders him from the house. This *volte face* can be mistakenly put down to disgust at the discovery that he has not killed his father after all, but no such ghoulish motivation is called for if her natural reaction to the jeers and giggles of the other girls is underlined. Pegeen has been exceedingly brusque, not only with the Widow Quin, but also with her contemporaries, when they come to the shop and threaten her monopoly of the young man.

I've no starch for the like of you, and let you walk on now to Killamuck.

In answer to Christy's boast that they have come four miles to see him, she says:

That lot came over the river, lepping the stones. It's not three perches when you go like that.

From there she goes on to warn him that they go out walking with the peelers, and would enjoy nothing better than to see him swinging at the end of a rope.

What joys would they have [asks Christy] to bring hanging to the likes of me?

It's queer joys they have, and who knows the thing they'd do, if it'd make the green stones cry itself to think of you swaying and swiggling at the butt of a rope, and you with a fine stout neck, God bless you! the way you'd be half an hour, in great anguish, getting your death.

From which outburst of threats and verbal pyrotechnics the good construction of this play becomes apparent—a sequence of events that discloses in Synge a new-found knowledge of the stage and its tricks. By getting Pegeen out to chase goats, the stage is cleared for Sean Keogh's attempt to bribe Christy to go away. This in turn is followed by the blandishments of the widow, which terminate in the spectacular arrival of the supposedly dead man himself. From which point the audience begins to discover for the first time the real harmlessness of the Playboy.

Not working at all? asks the Widow.

The divil a work, or if he did itself, you'd see him raising up a haystack like the stalk of a rush, or driving our last cow till he broke her leg at the hip, and when he wasn't at that he'd be fooling over little birds he had—finches and felts—or making mugs at his own self in the bit of a glass we had hung on the wall.

What way was he so foolish? It was running wild after the girls maybe?

Running wild, is it? If he seen a red petticoat coming swinging over the hill, he'd be off to hide in the sticks, and you'd see him shooting out his sheep's eyes between the little twigs and the leaves, and his two ears rising like a hare looking out through a gap. Girls, indeed!

In some of this abuse of the recessive by the dominant, one may well wonder whether we are not hearing some overtone— some amusing echo of the attitude of the big brothers: the land agent, the engineer, the Chinese missionary—toward young John Millington, the poet and friend of tramps. The fact that Synge loves Christy and provides that in the denouement of the last act he shall find himself, and triumph even over a possible marriage, supports this autobiographical suggestion for what it is worth. As is so often the way when a man grows big enough to win the woman of his dreams, he may discover that he is now too big to want her. Christy is a likely lad, and under the adoring applause of a clatch of girls he is quite capable of winning a horse race on the strand, and proceeding from this feat to a love scene, which for dignity and eloquence is probably unequaled in Irish literature—although it must be admitted that good love scenes are few and far between.

And let it be noted in this age when there are no holds barred on the screen, and precious few on the stage, that amongst the similarities between this scene and some of Shakespeare's— notably those in *Antony and Cleopatra*—is the absence of physical contact. In Shakespeare's case there is, of course, a special reason for this. In the case of Synge's play the reason for this restraint lies in the fact that both parties are discovering for the first time unplumbed depths of emotion in themselves that they had never experienced before. In the United States it is difficult sometimes to explain to a young actor and actress that they do not rush into each other's arms in this scene, in a manner worthy of the lines. The fact that they do not touch each other—apart from a tentative arm around a waist—is not an expression of prudery, but of the terrifying joy of an entirely new experience for both of them. All of this adds reason and point to the two major reversals in the last act—Old Mahon's delight in his newly aggressive son, and Pegeen's violent response to the laughter of the other girls.

It is Philly Cullen—the nasty suspicious neighbor—who follows Old Mahon on his way to the poorhouse, intending to beat him if he is crazy, and to bring him back to beat Christy if he is not. And followed by the girls, he bursts in upon the lovers. It is the girls—even more than the spectacle of Christy groveling at his father's feet and being beaten like a puppy— that drive Pegeen into her frenzy.

"Ask Pegeen to aid you [shouts Sara Tansey]. Her like does often change."

. . . . Now the world will see him pandied [says Pegeen venomously], and he an ugly liar was playing off the hero, and the fright of men.

What else can a new-found Christy do but attempt the deed again to justify himself, from which gesture follows the two final discoveries of his graduation. First, that he can make his old father run for his life, and second, that the company takes a very different view of a romantic tale from the far south and an attempted murder committed before their eyes.

I'll say, a strange man is a marvel with his mighty talk; but what's a squabble in your back yard, and the blow of a loy have taught me that there's a great gap between a gallous story and a dirty deed.

This time they all turn upon him as if prepared to lynch him. And, from this situation the widow offers him escape, which he refuses in the speech that got the company arrested for indecency in Philadelphia.

[37]

Come on [says the widow], and you'll be no worse than you were last night; and you with a double murder this time to be telling the girls.

I'll not leave Pegeen Mike.

. . . . Come on, I tell you, and I'll find you finer sweethearts at each waning moon.

It's Pegeen, I'm seeking only, and what'd I care if you brought me a drift of chosen females, standing in their shifts itself, maybe, from this place to the eastern world.

But when Pegeen returns, it is to lead the pack of terrified locals to rope him like a steer, while she burns him on the leg with a red-hot turf, in order to loosen his grip on the hearth.

Old Mahon, however, is still not dead. Indeed, he is alive for the first time to these spirited developments in his son, and is charmed with him on this account. As he loosens the ropes that have been twined around his son, he administers his fatherly curse on the whole community.

. . . my son and myself will be going our own way, and we'll have great times from this out telling stories of the villainy of Mayo, and the fools is here. Come on now.

To which Christy responds more generously

Ten thousand blessings upon all that's here, for you've turned me a likely gaffer in the end of all, the way I'll go romancing through a romping lifetime from this hour to the dawning of the judgment day.

This is a remark that turns them neither into fools nor villains, but that motivates the triumphant departure of the Mahon family, leaving to poor Pegeen the curtain line of many an Irish heroine:

Oh my grief, I've lost him surely. I've lost the only Playboy of the Western World.

The play can easily be performed in such a way as to justify fully the objections of the Gaelic League to it as a picture of home life in the west of Ireland. My point is that this is not the way in which it ought to be performed; nor is it the way in which the author intended it to be performed. That he had every intention of scoffing at certain religious susceptibilities and rogueries there is no doubt; but that he had any wish to denigrate the people of the boreens who were the love and target of his art—the friends and companions of his brief middle age—is simply absurd. In support of which is the fact that no complaints about Synge ever came from them. They came from middle-class circles in Dublin and in Cork, the type of people like Holloway, who could write:

"Synge is the evil genius of the Abbey, and Yeats his able lieutenant. Both dabble in the unhealthy."

So, too, Holloway's account of the riot shows his usual unreliability. The objections to the play did not come from Trinity College, but from the National University. There were Trinity boys in the stalls, but they did not come to suppress the performance, but to have a fight with the interruptors. As for Synge's own program note, in which he attempted to pacify objections by alleging that the whole plot of *The Playboy* was factual, what could be better calculated to make matters worse? It provides just another instance of the danger of authors attempting to explain themselves, or intervening in the quarrels that they have stirred up. They should leave that task to others—as Behan did.

Tired, perhaps, of perpetual controversy over his themes and topics, Synge decided after the *Playboy* disturbance to write an unimpeachable epic play on the safest of all subjects—the Deirdre legend. This has been a favorite subject for Irish writers, particularly dramatists, since the dawning of a general interest in Gaelic literature in the latter part of the nineteenth century. Indeed there was a time when Deirdre plays seemed to be becoming a public nuisance. We have Yeats's

[39]

Deirdre and one by George Russell. We have Lyle Donaghy's *Deirdre* and Donagh MacDonagh's—to mention a few of the more successful. There is even a cantata by Rolleston and Esposito, and there are about nine Scottish variants.

Like most of the Gaelic mythological material, the story shows more character and touches of humor than is usual in the sagas of other countries. It also displays a peculiarly Irish attitude toward women that has not been sufficiently remarked upon by scholars when editing the material. Forgetting O'Casey's lamentable juveniles, it is fair to say that when the great majority of good Irish dramatists come to depict the ripe young Irish female, they do not as a rule show her as a Ministering-Angel-Thou, but basically, as a killer.

I do not mean by this that she is a murderess. Indeed she would probably be the last person to recognize any lethal urges in herself. It just happens that, as a rule, she inspires her gentlemen friends to acts of violence that usually end in some form of disaster.

This view of Irish girlhood is, of course, an unjust one. As a class they are charming, and very enjoyable—if somewhat cynical—company, which last characteristic they attribute, quite fairly, to their experiences with Irish men. But it is the men who, on the whole, have written the plays and poems and have created the image of Deirdre, which is now inseparably linked to the celebrated prototype, provided by Yeats's Madame Gonne MacBride.

Deirdre—a *femme fatale* of proportions comparable to those of Hedda Gabler—is the death not only of Naisi, but also of his two *fidèles*, and the fact that she concludes the holocaust by adding her own body to the heap on the stage is only another indication of her honesty of purpose, and of her enormous concern with violent death. Deirdre is a character who is not alone in her interest in such matters. She is a charter member of an order whose Abbess is Cathleen ni Houlihan herself.

Those that are red-cheeked now
Will be white-cheeked tomorrow.

This view of women not only illuminates the very Irish ending of *Playboy*—in the course of which the men escape to other pastures. It also is to be found in the difference between the Shavian ending of Pygmalion, and America's conclusion to *My Fair Lady*—where Professor Higgins is dutifully hung in the closet, without anybody even paying him the compliment of feeling so sad.

But the story of Deirdre has other attractions beside the opportunities that it offers for depicting a powerful woman. It has many similarities to the legend of Tristan and Isolde— the conflict of the old man with the young man for the hand of the girl. It is repeated again in the Fenian Cycle under the guise of Dairmuid and Grania—not to mention *The Iliad*, itself. It has also an element in it that gives expression to one of the most familiar problems of adolescence—Shall I take a safe job in Father's business, or run off somewhere, and give voice to my soul?

Most young men of spirit and originality pass through this phase between the ages of about eighteen and twenty-five, and what they are in fact asking themselves is whether they prefer to elope with their Muse, flinging all else to the winds, or should they be sensible, and maybe spend the rest of their lives wondering what would have happened if they had not. The nub of the problem lies, of course, in the question as to whether or not their Muse is a fraud. Maybe a few years with Deirdre will make all last acts, however disastrous, worth while. It certainly did in Synge's case, but then Synge's Muse was not his only killer, and from an early age he had known that his life would be a short one.

The company of Maire O'Neill provided Synge with some comfort and excitement during his last weeks in the nursing home in which he died in 1909. Here she visited him nearly every day, and told him the gossip of the theater and received his instructions for her own reading. He was determined to educate her, a fact that she took in good part, whether or not she actually studied her assignments. He felt that death was coming, although probably not so soon.

> I've thirty months, and that's my pride,
> Before my age's a double score,
> Though many lively men have died
> At twenty-nine or little more.

He actually had only six months to live when he wrote this. But before the ghoulish rituals that were to attend upon his interment, he had this other play to finish—or half finish—*Deirdre of the Sorrows.*

This is usually described as an unfinished play. It is true that he had the script with him in the nursing home where he died, and where he was supposed to be fiddling with it. As finally pushed into shape by Yeats and Lady Gregory it was sufficiently complete to be performed, and it displays in action much greater dramatic values than are to be found in most of the other versions. Written in Synge's personal vernacular, rather than in verse, it asserts its nationality, and avoids the dangers inherent in most costume pieces of this type. What can be said against it—and what would probably have been his principal concern in a rewrite—is, of all things, a tendency to plagiarize himself. But, after all, who better could Synge plagiarize?

It is difficult to conceive what sort of a love scene a dramatist could write after having put everything he felt on the subject into the passages in *The Playboy.* There is much to indicate that Synge was experiencing this very difficulty, as his faculties hesitated on his deathbed.

It's a poor thing to be so lonesome you'd squeeze kisses on a cur dog's nose.

. . . you'll have great sport one day seeing Naisi getting a harshness in his two sheep's eyes and he looking on yourself.

And is it you who go around in the woods making the thrushes bear a grudge against the hearers of the sweetness of your voice. . . .

Deirdre is not Synge's creation. She is an earlier bard's woman—if indeed she is a woman at all and not a transvestite. Why Synge wrote this last play at all is a mystery so far as the heroic trappings are concerned. Maybe he wanted to get away from the noble peasant and into the good graces of the Irish-Irelanders. Or perhaps he had an urge to return in the major key to the theme of his first play—the old man, the young man, and the faithless bride—and end it in more acceptable terms than in a friendly fireside talk between the rivals, while Deirdre is turned out to tramp the bogs with Owen.

Synge's merits as a poet have been obscured to some extent by his greater fame as a playwright, and by the contemporary greatness of W. B. Yeats. None of his verse can approach the ecstatic qualities of his folk-prose. Nevertheless it is full of statement—a factor that may be the worst thing about it in modern eyes. Take, for instance, the short piece entitled "A Wish," in which he gives expression to the subtle and timely idea that joy, perhaps, is not enough, and that he would endow his beloved with more than birthday presents.

> May seven tears in every week
> Touch the hollow of your cheek,
> That I—signed with such a dew—
> For a lion's share may sue
> Of the roses ever curled
> Round the May-pole of the world.
> Heavy riddles lie in this,
> Sorrow's sauce for every kiss.

A more serious flaw than the uncertainty in the beat, is the fact that the lucidity of the first two lines is then obscured by four lines of mixed imagery of almost record proportions.

[43]

Signed by dew, he may then take legal proceedings to obtain a lion's share of roses, curled around the world's Maypole. Certainly heavy riddles lie here. But not all of Synge's verse has this inappropriate confusion of sorrow with a sauce. There is his apostrophe to the oaks of Glencree—the true, unchanging love in whose final embrace his marriage will be consummated. What could be more characteristic of the ways of Synge's thought?

> My arms are round you, and I lean
> Against you, while the lark
> Sings over us, and golden lights, and green
> Shadows are on your bark.
> There'll come a season when you'll stretch
> Black boards to cover me:
> Then in Mount Jerome I will lie, poor wretch,
> With worms eternally.

The fourth volume of his *Collected Works* consists of essays and articles contributed to periodical publications between 1904 and 1907—principally *The Shanachie* (a Dublin literary magazine) and *The Manchester Guardian*. They are all vivid and informative descriptions of the vagrants and farmers of Wicklow, Kerry, and the Congested Districts of the west. Sometimes (as in the case of "The Vagrants of Wicklow") the original essay has been rewritten for the *Collected Works*, and sometimes significant passages have been left out altogether, possibly by other hands, as already mentioned.

Throughout these essays we find a recurrence of the same theme; that there is this similarity between the peasantry and the middle class—the gifted son is always the poorest, "usually a writer or artist with no sense for speculation—and in a family of peasants, where the average comfort is just over penury, the gifted son sinks also, and is soon a tramp on the roadside."

I know that they, or most of them in their hearts despise a man of letters

he wrote to his Molly, when describing his family.

Success in life is what they aim for, and they understand no success that does not bring a nice house, and servants and good dinners. You're not like that are you?

And then he adds to his Changeling—as he called her—"I hope you'll read steadily while I'm away."

The social and intellectual gulf between them, of which, as an Anglo-Irishman, he was fully aware, is emphasized by his insistence that she allow him to educate her, and by a romantic whimsy that she was, perhaps, the offspring of a mansion, grander than his own Crosthwaite Park, who had been stolen away by the fairies. Maybe she was not just a shopgirl, but a lost child of noble parentage. There is an opera on this theme— *The Bohemian Girl*—with which they were both doubtless acquainted. But although Molly was in many ways a bohemian, it is not easy to picture her breaking into: "I dreamt that I dwelt in marble halls." This awareness of caste on Synge's part was not inconsistent with a complete absence of patronizing humbug in his treatment of the peasant and of folk material. He could be a folk writer without being folksy, and although his picture of a people whom he loved is not flattering, it is both good-humored and understanding—a fact that was widely appreciated.

Molly played his Deirdre after his death, and eventually married—not the harmless rival whom he had always feared, Udolphus Wright, but a man called Mair, by whom she had a daughter whom she named Pegeen. Eventually she married Arthur Sinclair—the Michael James Flaherty of *Playboy*—in and out of whose company she concluded a long, stormy professional career. Their fellow Irish Players used to allege that it was best for all when they were not on speaking terms.

It was difficult for hands unknown to fiddle with much of Synge's works after his death, as most of it was already in print, thanks largely to George Roberts—"Maunsel and Company"—a man who had played small parts in the early Abbey Company and who afterward became the only distinguished Irish publisher of his day. This is the man upon whose head James Joyce subsequently poured out quantities of dull auto-biographical abuse over the contract for *Dubliners*. On the slender basis of six plays, most of them one-acters, Synge laid the foundation of what, until the coming of O'Casey, was to be the world-wide reputation of the Abbey Theatre. It is a pity that so much of his other memorabilia was suppressed and even destroyed before it could be rescued by Stephens. Like the mosaics of Sancta Sophia much of his color was covered for many years with unnecessary whitewash.

Indeed, the circumstances surrounding his funeral provide the most striking illustration of the attitude of his nearest and dearest toward the literary and theatrical connections of this brilliant cuckoo in their nest. In some respects it recalls the macabre, hushed-up obsequies of the errant son of the Emperor Franz Josef, except that, here, there was no hunting lodge, no suicide, and the lady-in-the-case was a respectable fiancée who was considerably more celebrated than the grim-faced family.

A request from Yeats that a death mask be made was brusquely turned down, and the cortege to Mount Jerome was strictly limited to a few neighbors and relatives. No flowers were accepted from outsiders, and most of the expressions of sympathy from various parts of the world remained unacknowledged. But at the gates of the cemetery the Abbey Company was waiting, and accompanied by other loyal but uninvited admirers, they followed the remains of John Synge to its final resting place.

And presently, when the clatter of cabs on their way back to Kingstown had died away up the road, they all went home, leaving many unauthorized blooms on the earth that still covers him.

[46]

SELECTED BIBLIOGRAPHY

NOTE: *The most exhaustive catalogue of the published work of Synge, covering editions on both sides of the Atlantic together with a list of his numerous contributions to periodicals, is to be found in Appendix A to Maurice Bourgeois's book, listed below. This appendix also contains a list of translations down to 1913, and the best set of references to critical works and articles about the writer prior to the same date.*

A useful but abbreviated bibliography of Synge's works appears in the book by Greene and Stephens, which, however, contains no reference to works or outside comment on Synge himself.

The standard edition of his Collected Plays and Other Writings *is that published in Dublin by Maunsell and Co. in 1910. (This is actually the second collected edition.)* Plays by John M. Synge *is the title of a further edition, issued by Allen and Unwin in London in 1932. Some single plays were published by Luce in Boston in 1911, and are not mentioned by Bourgeois.*

The text of all the plays and also The Aran Islands *is at present available in the United States in paperback form, and there is a one-volume collected edition of the plays issued in paperback by Vintage. A new Oxford University Press edition of the* Complete Works *edited by Ann Saddlemyer is at present in the course of preparation.*

References to Synge and his works are to be found passim *in the various Introductions to the anthologies collected by John Gassner, and also in the theatrical surveys of Allardyce Nicoll. There are many contemporary references to Synge in* The Letters of W. B. Yeats, *edited by Allan Wade, and in George Moore's "Hail and Farewell." T. R. Henn includes some consideration of Synge in his work "The Harvest of Tragedy," where* Playboy *is discussed as a tragedy.*

"An Inaugural Dissertation on John Millington Synge" was submitted to the University of Bonn by Herbert Frenzel "as a contribution to Irish folk lore and to the Psychology of Primitive Tribes," and published in Duren in 1932. ("In the Channel Islands we find the same burning of seaweed.")

[47]

Bickley, Francis. J. M. Synge and the Irish Dramatic Movement. London, Constable, 1912.

Bourgeois, Maurice. John Millington Synge and the Irish Theatre. London, Constable, 1912.

Boyd, Ernest. The Contemporary Drama of Ireland. Boston, Little, Brown, 1917.

Corkery, Daniel. Synge and Anglo-Irish Literature. Cork, Cork University Press, 1931.

Coxhead, Elizabeth. J. M. Synge and Lady Gregory. London, The British Council, 1952.

Greene, David H., and Edward M. Stephens. J. M. Synge 1871–1909. New York, Macmillan, 1959.

Howarth, Herbert. The Irish Writers 1880–1940. London, Rockliffe, 1958.

Malone, Andrew E. The Irish Drama. London, Constable, 1929.

Mercier, Vivian. The Irish Comic Tradition. New York, Oxford University Press, 1962.

Morgan, A. E. Tendencies of Modern English Drama. London, Constable, 1924.

O'Connor, Frank. Synge in "The Irish Theatre." (A series of lectures edited by Lennox Robinson.) London, Macmillan, 1938.

Robinson, Lennox. Curtain Up. London, Joseph, 1942.

——— Ireland's Abbey Theatre. London, Sedgwick and Jackson, 1951.

Strong, L. A. G. John Millington Synge. London, Allen and Unwin, 1941.

Synge, Rev. Samuel. Letters to My Daughter. Dublin, Talbot Press, 1931.

Taylor, Estella Ruth. The Modern Irish Writers. Lawrence, Kansas University Press, 1954.

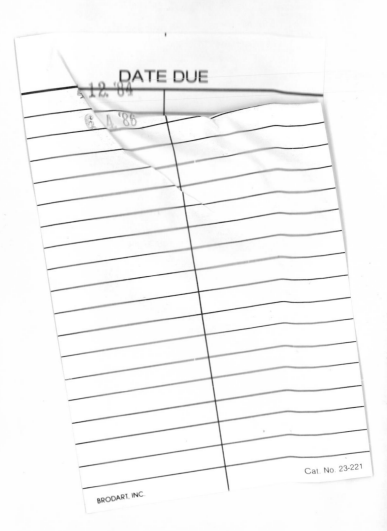